# Alligator or Crocodile?

## A Compare and Contrast Book

by Jennifer Shields

Alligators and crocodiles are reptiles. They are members of a group called crocodilians. Caimans and gharials are also crocodilians.

If you look closely, you will notice differences between them.

There are two species of alligators, two gharials, and six caimans.

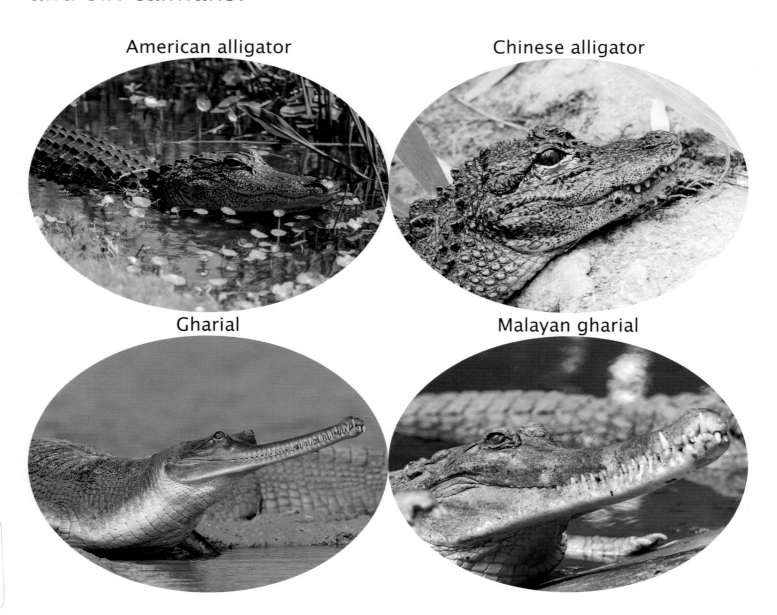

American alligator

Chinese alligator

Gharial

Malayan gharial

Black caiman

Broad-snouted caiman

Cuvier's dwarf caiman

Schneider's smooth-fronted caiman

Spectacled caiman

Yacarè caiman

There are fourteen species of crocodiles.

The American alligator and American crocodile are the only crocodilians native to North America.

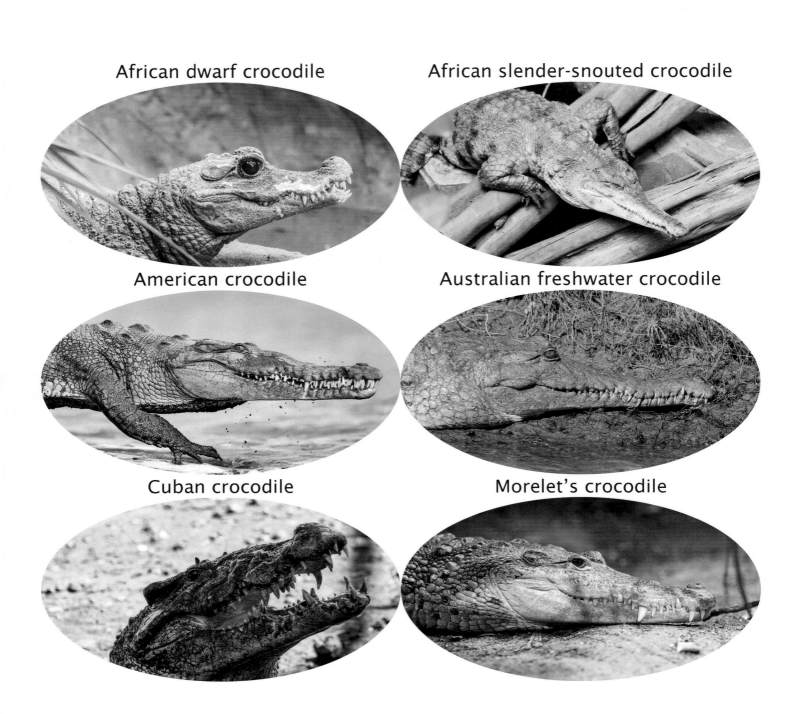

African dwarf crocodile

African slender-snouted crocodile

American crocodile

Australian freshwater crocodile

Cuban crocodile

Morelet's crocodile

Mugger crocodile

New Guinea freshwater crocodile

Nile crocodile

Orinoco crocodile

Philippine crocodile

Saltwater crocodile

Siamese crocodile

West African crocodile

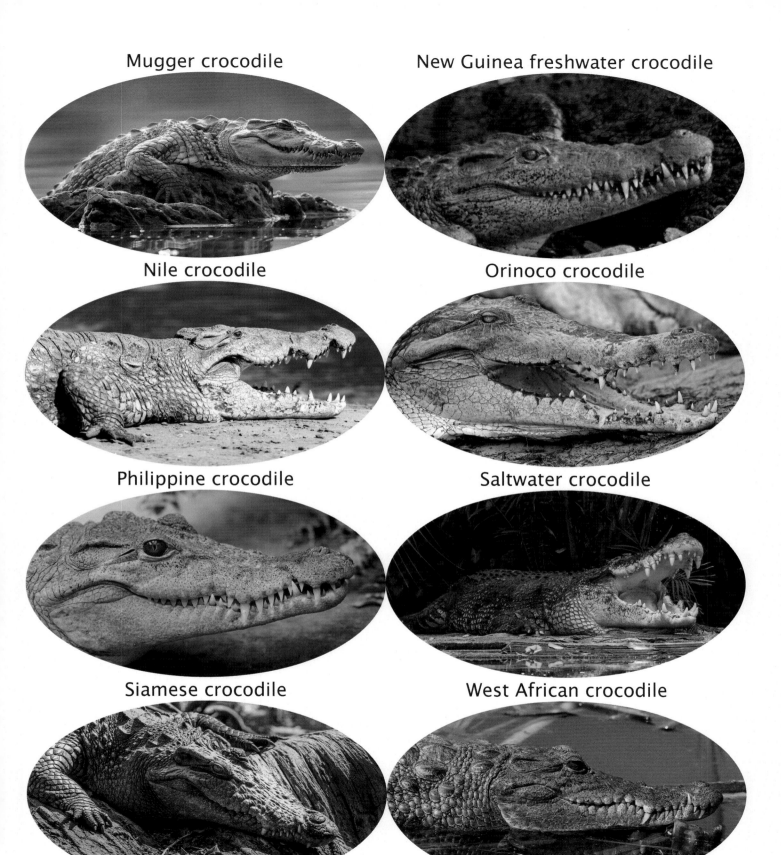

American alligator

As cold-blooded reptiles, crocodilians need warm temperatures to be active. They bask in the sun to warm up.

Both alligators and crocodiles live on land and in water.

eye

ear

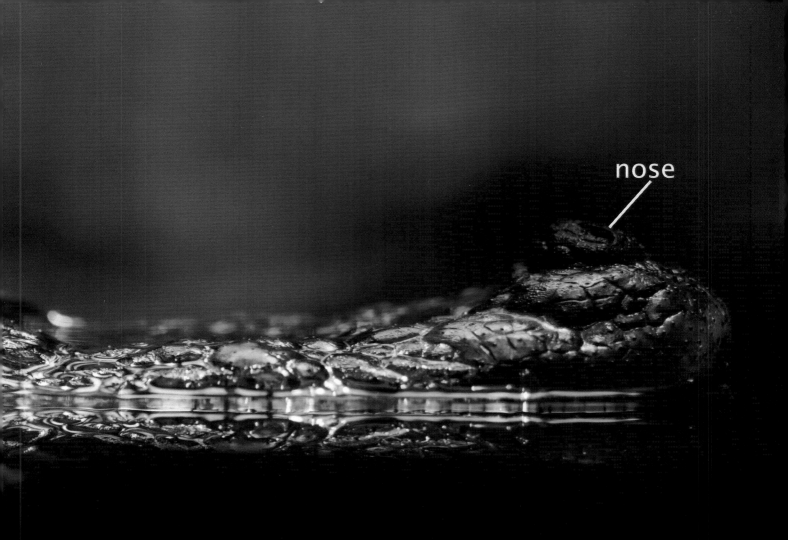

nose

They have a third eyelid called a nictitating membrane. These eyelids are clear like goggles to protect their eyes so they can see underwater.

They can keep most of their body under the water to hide from prey. Their eyes, ears, and nose are on the top of their heads and can be above water to see, hear, and breathe.

Nile crocodiles

Nile crocodiles

Nile crocodiles

Both female alligators and crocodiles build nests on land to lay their eggs. Unlike most reptiles, crocodilian moms guard their nests and protect their babies after they hatch. They will gently carry their newly-hatched babies in their mouths to the water.

American alligators

Both alligators and crocodiles eat fish, turtles, birds, and small mammals. Nile crocodiles will also eat larger mammals like giraffes and wildebeests!

In general, male crocodilians are larger than females. The smallest crocodilian is the Cuvier's dwarf and the largest is the saltwater crocodile. The American alligator is in the middle.

*How long might each of the crocodilians grow?*

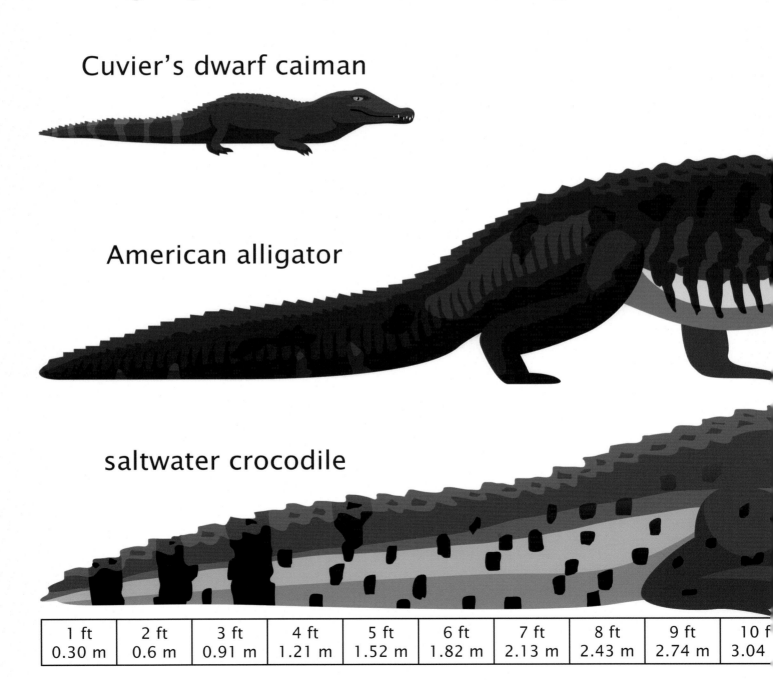

Cuvier's dwarf caiman

American alligator

saltwater crocodile

| 1 ft | 2 ft | 3 ft | 4 ft | 5 ft | 6 ft | 7 ft | 8 ft | 9 ft | 10 f |
|---|---|---|---|---|---|---|---|---|---|
| 0.30 m | 0.6 m | 0.91 m | 1.21 m | 1.52 m | 1.82 m | 2.13 m | 2.43 m | 2.74 m | 3.04 |

How tall are you? How does that compare to the length of these crocodilians?

How does it compare to an adult in your life?

| | |
|---|---|
| 7 ft | 2.13 m |
| 6 ft | 1.82 m |
| 5 ft | 1.52 m |
| 4 ft | 1.21 m |
| 3 ft | 0.91 m |
| 2 ft | 0.6 m |
| 1 ft | 0.30 m |

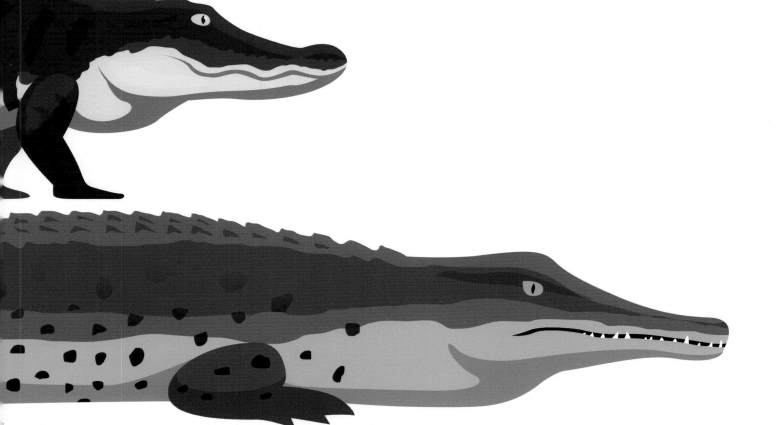

| 1 ft | 12 ft | 13 ft | 14 ft | 15 ft | 16 ft | 17 ft | 18 ft | 19 ft | 20 ft |
|---|---|---|---|---|---|---|---|---|---|
| 35 m | 3.65 m | 3.96 m | 4.26 m | 4.57 m | 4.87 m | 5.18 m | 5.48 m | 5.79 m | 6.09 m |

Alligators generally have dark skin.
Crocodiles generally have lighter skin.

American alligator

Orinoco crocodile

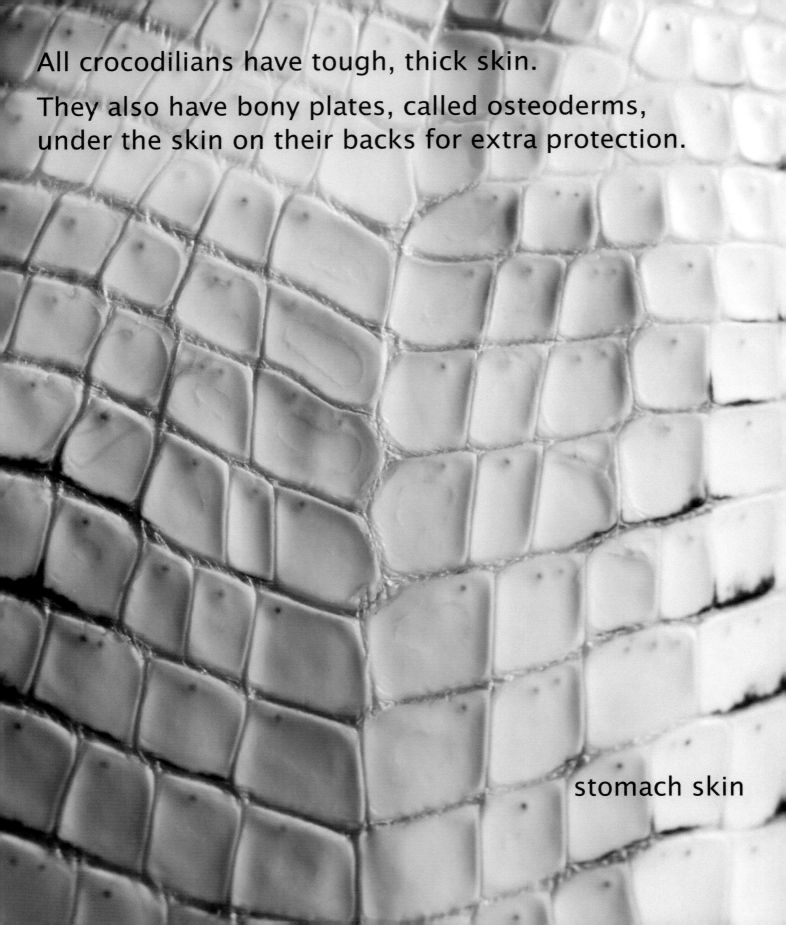

All crocodilians have tough, thick skin.

They also have bony plates, called osteoderms, under the skin on their backs for extra protection.

stomach skin

Alligators have large, wide snouts shaped like the letter "u."

American alligator

Most crocodiles have pointed "v-shaped" snouts like this Orinoco crocodile. But, of the fourteen crocodiles species, some, like the Mugger crocodile have broader muzzles.

Orinoco crocodile

When an alligator closes its mouth only the top teeth and maybe one bottom tooth on each side of the mouth will show.

American alligator

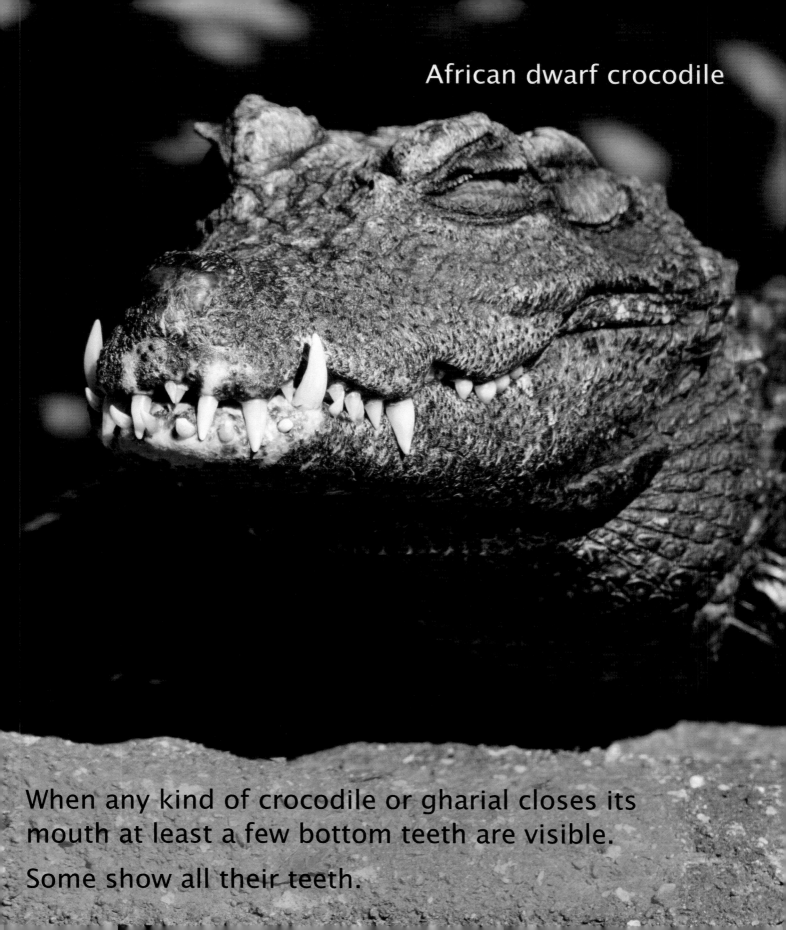

African dwarf crocodile

When any kind of crocodile or gharial closes its mouth at least a few bottom teeth are visible.

Some show all their teeth.

As they grow, both alligators and crocodiles replace their teeth with bigger teeth. It only takes a few days for a new tooth to grow in when one falls out.

*How long does it take for you to replace a lost tooth?*

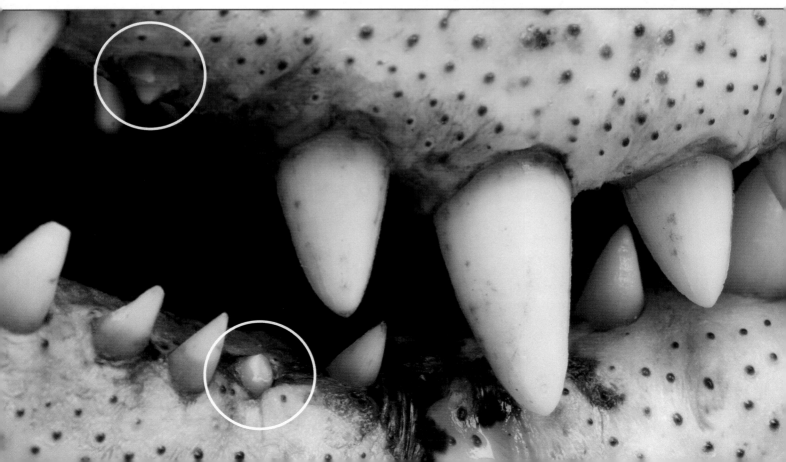

American alligator

Both have strong tails for swimming. They can even use them to jump out of the water!

saltwater crocodile

freshwater crocodile

Crocodilian feet have both claws and webs to help them move on land and in the water.

American alligator

# For Creative Minds

## True or False?

Using what you read in the book, determine whether these statements are true or false.

| | |
|---|---|
| **1** There are 14 different species of alligators and 2 crocodiles. | **2** Five species of crocodilians are native to North America. |
| **3** Cold-blooded alligators and crocodiles bask in the sun to warm themselves. | **4** All reptiles lay eggs and the young survive purely on instinct. |
| **5** All alligators and crocodiles have tough, thick sink. | **6** In general, alligators have large, wide snouts. Many crocodiles have long pointed snouts but there is variation between species. |
| **7** If an alligator or crocodile loses a tooth, it will never grow back. | **8** Alligators and crocodiles have webbed feet to help them move through water and claws to help them move on land. |

Answers: 1-False: There are 14 species of crocodiles and 2 alligators. 2-False: American alligators and American crocodiles are the only crocodilians that are native to North America. 3-True. 4-False: Most, but not all reptiles, lay eggs and the young survive on instinct. Alligator and crocodile moms protect and raise their young. 5-True. 6-True. 7-False: It just takes a few days for a new tooth to grow back! 8-True.

# Match the Adaptation

All living things have adaptations that help them survive in their habitat. Match the photo of alligator and crocodile adaptations to the description.

1. Alligators and crocodiles have a third, clear eyelid (nictitating membrane) that helps them see underwater.

2. Mothers care for, protect, and raise their young.

3. Since they are cold-blooded, they bask in the sun to warm up.

4. They hide from potential prey by hiding most of their body underwater and keep their eyes, ears, and noses above water.

5. They have both webs and claws on their feet to help them move in water and on land.

6. Strong tails help push them through the water and even let them jump to grab prey.

A
B
C
D
E
F

Answers: 1C; 2F; 3A; 4B; 5E; 6D

To my late husband, David Leadingham, who encouraged me to be brave and try new adventures—JS

Thanks to John Brueggen, Director of the St. Augustine Alligator Farm Zoological Park, for verifying the information in this book and for his photograph of the New Guinea freshwater crocodile. All other photographs are licensed through Adobe Stock Photos or Shutterstock.

Library of Congress Cataloging-in-Publication Data

Names: Shields, Jennifer, 1960- author.
Title: Alligator or crocodile? : a compare and contrast book / by Jennifer Shields.
Description: Mt. Pleasant, SC : Arbordale Publishing, LLC, [2023] | Includes bibliographical references.
Identifiers: LCCN 2022036988 (print) | LCCN 2022036989 (ebook) | ISBN 9781643519821 (paperback) | ISBN 9781638170013 (interactive dual-language, read along) | ISBN 9781638170396 (epub) | ISBN 9781638170204 (adobe pdf)
Subjects: LCSH: Alligators--Juvenile literature. | Crocodiles--Juvenile literature.
Classification: LCC QL666.C925 S5425 2023 (print) | LCC QL666.C925 (ebook) | DDC 597.98/2--dc23/eng/20220803
LC record available at https://lccn.loc.gov/2022036988
LC ebook record available at https://lccn.loc.gov/2022036989

Translated into Spanish: *¿Aligátor o cocodrilo?*
Spanish paperback ISBN: 9781638172628
Spanish ePub ISBN: 9781638172802
Spanish PDF ebook ISBN: 9781638172741
Dual-language read along available online through www.fathomreads.com

English Lexile® Level: 640L

Bibliography

"American Alligator: Species Profile - Everglades National Park (U.S. National Park Service)." Nps.gov, 2016, www.nps.gov/ever/learn/nature/alligator.htm.
David, Johnathan. Alligator vs Crocodile: All 9 Differences Explained – Everything Reptiles. www.everythingreptiles.com/alligator-vs-crocodile/#3_Crocodiles_Have_V-Shaped_Snouts.
Reptile Guide. Stacey, July 20,2021. Alligator Teeth Explained: Facts, Cost, and More! reptile.guide/alligator-teeth

Printed in the USA
This product conforms to CPSIA 2008

Arbordale Publishing, LLC
Mt. Pleasant, SC 29464
www.ArbordalePublishing.com